Virginia

INTERACTIVE

NOTEBOOK

By Carole Marsh

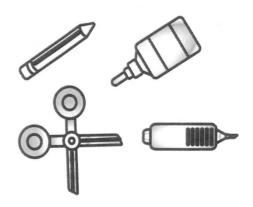

WORD FROM THE AUTHOR

Dear Teacher,

This book is your guide to using Interactive Notebooks for Virginia state studies!

Included are hands-on, reproducible activities to teach your students about Virginia geography, history, people, events, government, economics, state symbols, and more. Also included is a step-by-step guide to the Interactive Notebook concept.

Your students and you are sure to have a great time and a fabulous year, learning about our amazing state with this fun, creative, effective approach.

I'd love to hear from you on Facebook, Pinterest, or by email, and to see pictures of your students' work!

Best regards,

Carole Marsh

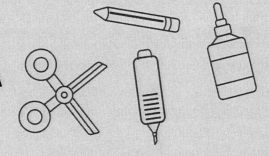

ABLE OF CONTENTS

WHY USE INTERACTIVE NOTEBOOKS?

Interactive Notebooks are great for students!

- Building an Interactive Notebook helps students build organization skills as they take responsibility for their learning resources.

- The Interactive Notebook provides students with an outlet to apply the knowledge they gain in ways that express their own ideas and creativity.

- Guided writing activities incorporated into an Interactive Notebook help your students develop into independent, creative, reflective thinkers.

- And, once completed, an Interactive Notebook becomes a comprehensive and engaging review tool to help your students master content and prepare for tests.

Interactive Notebooks are great for teachers!

- You can easily customize your instruction.

- You direct the learning process and pace.

- You determine where to dig deeper...and when and where to add pizzazz!

- You choose which projects to use as instruction, which projects to use as reinforcement, which projects to use as independent practice, and which projects to use as assessments.

- You can supplement activities with your own texts and projects.

- And, you meet the unique needs of your students—in each and every year!

Let's get started!

WHAT'S NEEDED FOR INTERACTIVE NOTEBOOKING?

What Students Need:

- a spiral-bound composition book (each student needs his or her own book)
  (spiral-bound books that are slightly larger than 8.5x11 are ideal for Interactive Notebooks)

- scissors, crayons or colored pencils, highlighters, glue/glue-sticks, pencils

- brad-style fasteners (needed for two activities)

- access to reference sources you approve for research
  (e.g., books in your classroom, library materials, and supervised use of Internet, per your school policy)

Remember, Interactive Notebooks will be creative and colorful, but not all students are great artists, and that's OK. The benefits of Interactive Notebooking are not in perfect coloring, cutting, and folding. They are in the interactive approach to learning; the pride students take in their work; the deeper connection they develop to the topics they study; and the creativity, mindfulness, and reflection that go into their work. In fact, gluing down a foldable, only to then realize it's upside down, is part of the learning process—and not the end of the world! So, recognize their efforts, where they shine in their own unique ways, and the learning that occurs.

What Teachers Need:

- access to a copier or printer, plus paper and toner (or a copy allowance)

- back-up supplies in case students need them

- classroom reference materials for students to use as needed

- **Just as importantly, you'll need a plan and activities that are designed for the Interactive Notebook process. *That's where we come in!***

This book provides you with an effective plan, plus loads of activities that are designed specifically to be used as part of an Interactive Notebook. You also get a variety of writing prompts, activity extensions, and reflection ideas—one or more for each activity. We've provided a "Let's Learn About Virginia" get-started letter for students that explains the basic Interactive Notebooking benefits, organization, and expectations. Adapt or use as is; just add your supply list to the back. There's even a rubric for easy Interactive Notebook grading. And it's all easily adaptable and customizable in any way you choose.

How to Create an Interactive Notebook

Step 1: Every book needs a cover!
Students can illustrate their Interactive Notebook covers with a collage of pictures that represent Virginia to them. Possibilities include the state name, a map, their own picture, sports teams, nature scenes, state symbols, or anything else they select. Students can glue pictures directly to the cover or to a separate sheet of paper that they then glue to the cover. Wrap several pieces of clear packing tape across the cover to hold it together and protect it throughout the year.

Step 2: Personalize Page One
Students should write their name, how long they have lived in Virginia, what they love about Virginia, and places in Virginia they have visited.

Step 3: Stay organized with a Table of Contents (TOC)
Students should write "Table of Contents" on the top of pages 2-5 (or 2-7 if you plan to add supplemental material). This sets aside space for students to record page numbers and page topics as they build their Interactive Notebook throughout the year.

The activities in this book are designed as "spreads" where a left and right page are used for the same topic. You can allow students to list each spread/topic on one line of the TOC if you follow this concept.

Students should write a page number on the outside bottom corner of each page. This will make it easy for them to find a page they are looking for.

Tip: When you make an assignment, write the TOC entry on your whiteboard, and have students record it in their TOC first. That way, they can flip back for a reminder of what goes on what page.

Step 4: Kick off each unit with a KWL Chart
A good way to launch each new unit in the Interactive Notebook is for students to create a unit page that includes a KWL chart. This gives students a chance to think about the upcoming topic in advance, encouraging them to participate in class discussion. Remind students to list their unit page and KWL in their TOC.

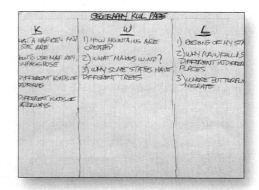

The activities in this resource are grouped into units by strand (geography, history, economics, etc.). You can adjust the order of the strands, combine strands, or move a few activities from one strand to another.

Tip: Do a notebook check soon after students create their KWLs, and you'll get insight into what students know and what they want to know, helping you customize your instruction.

Step 5: Every page deserves a title!

For any page whose activity does not include a title, students students should write a title across the top of the page. That will make it easier for them to find pages and to know at a glance what each page is about.

Tip: Build a "master" Interactive Notebook. Add activity pages as you assign them (you don't have to do them), and record extension/reflection assignments. Your notebook master will make notebook checks easy, and students can use it as a reference if they are absent or missing an assignment.

Step 6: Activities on the right

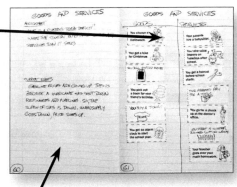

Most activities and foldables are designed to fit on one page, with the other side used for writing, reflecting, and expansion activities. Votes are in, and "activities on the right" is the winner!

(The right-hand page is easier to use because it usually has flat, unused pages underneath it. Plus, because most page-flipping is right to left, glued pages adhere better to right-hand pages.)

Step 7: Expand, write, and reflect (on the left)

Make more of each learning opportunity by pairing structured activities and foldables with writing, reflecting, and expansion activities. The left-hand page of each spread is your spot for these. We've included a list to go with every activity topic, and you're sure to come up with plenty more of your own! You have a lot of flexibility in how you use this space.

Occasionally, an activity is designed to go across the top of the two-page spread (e.g., timelines). When that occurs, students can do their writing assignment underneath.

Tip: Give students a standing assignment to write a sentence about how they are impacted by what they learned. Ideas include how it changed their perspective, how they can use it, and why it matters.

Step 8: A glossary is the perfect ending!

Students can build a glossary as they learn important terms throughout the year. Based on the number of pages you expect students to use in their composition books, you can suggest a reasonable number of pages for them to set aside as a glossary. Words can be listed under a letter heading in the order they are added. It's not easy to plan the right amount of space for each letter, but here are a few suggestions to help:

- 5 pages = 5 letters per page, except 6 on the last page
- 8 pages = 3 letters per page, except 5 on the last page
- less than 5 pages = not easy to alphabetize by even just one letter, but students could list key terms in the order they learn them, perhaps with unit headings for organization

Step 9: Feedback and positive reinforcement!

Show interest in your students' Interactive Notebooks to help them understand the importance of their work. Notebook checks help make sure students complete their work and make up anything they miss. A rubric at the end of this book provides a simple 10-point grading system. Feel free to customize and adapt to suit your needs. Positive reinforcement and recognition goes a long way!

Tip: Give students a copy of the rubric to put in their Interactive Notebook at the start of the year. They can use it to do self-checks throughout the year.

DETAILED ACTIVITY LIST
+ COPYING INSTRUCTIONS
& IDEAS FOR EXTENSION, WRITING, & REFLECTION
(i.e., LEFT-HAND PAGE ACTIVITIES)

Virginia GEOGRAPHY

Using Maps & Globes to Learn About Virginia 15-16
(copy both pages single-sided, each on their own sheet of paper)
Tip: Display a variety of different types of state maps for students to view.
- Describe 2-3 real-life scenarios that each require use of a different map.
- A "Geographic Information System" (GIS) allows you to access many different types of geographical data, select which data you are interested in, and view it on one map. Describe a scenario where a state GIS would be useful, and explain how it would help.

My Map of Virginia. 17-18
(copy this activity front-and-back)
Create a Virginia gazetteer of unique place names: Draw a vertical line down the center of a page. On the left side of the line, write down the names of at least 10 Virginia cities, waterways, or other geographic features that have interesting or unusual names. Then rewrite them on the right side in alphabetical order.

Virginia's Place in the United States/U.S. Regions. 19-20
(copy this activity front-and-back)
- Create a web diagram: Write your U.S. region in a center circle. Then write characteristics that define or describe your region in separate circles and connect them to the center.
- Research the highest point (elevation) in each state in your region. Write place names and elevations on a step diagram, from lowest to highest.

Virginia Regions 21
(copy this activity single-sided)
- You're hired!: Write a paragraph describing the region where you live for a promotional brochure aimed at attracting new residents and businesses.
- Describe the sights, sounds, smells, tastes, and feel of a Virginia region, but don't name the region. Let a classmate read your description and guess the region.

Virginia Climate 22
(copy this activity single-sided)
- Look up the definitions of "climate" and "weather" and write them in your glossary.
- Explain the difference between climate and weather. Then explain how they are related.
- Describe the local weather for the last week and how it affected you.

Virginia Agriculture 23
(copy this activity single-sided)
- How might weather negatively impact Virginia's top crops? Create a chart or diagram to explain the cause-and-effect chain of events that could occur.
- Research other types of agriculture that are successful in Virginia, and list them.

Virginia Nature 24
(copy this activity single-sided)
- Write a paragraph explaining why you think it is important or unimportant that Virginia have a state flower, state fish, state tree, etc.
- Research an endangered or at-risk animal in Virginia. List ideas to protect it.

Virginia Transportation

(copy this activity single-sided)
- Create a T chart listing advantages and disadvantages of one of Virginia's transportation systems. How might new technologies solve problems? How might they create drastic changes? Predict positive and negative effects.
- Plan a trip: Use a roadmap to plan a trip to another state. List all the roads you would take to drive to the state border, starting from your home or school.

Virginia HISTORY

(copy this activity single-sided)

Tip: Hand out this activity sheet periodically throughout the year, especially as you cover history. There are too many great Virginians to choose only one!
Do a creative writing project about this person. You could write a poem, a letter, a journal entry, a family tree, a 5-Ws chart, a newspaer article, a comic strip, a mini-biography, etc.

(copy this activity front-and-back)
- Draw or write something in the style of art of the American Indians in Virginia.
- Compare a ceremony used by your own cultural group with one used by a Virginia American Indian tribe. How are they similar? How are they different?

(copy both pages single-sided, each on their own sheet of paper)
Tip: Assign these activities together, even though they go on two spreads.
- Close your eyes and imagine being an early explorer in Virginia. Open your eyes and write a multi-sensory, descriptive journal entry to describe your experience.
- Draw a compass rose in the center of the page. Next to each of the eight points, list a reason why the area that is now Virginia was a difficult and dangerous place to explore hundreds of years ago.

(copy this activity front-and-back)
- Imagine what it would be like as a settler arriving in Virginia and meeting American Indians for the first time. Write a journal entry from your perspective. Then write a journal entry from the perspective of the American Indian you met.
- Look at a current political map of Virginia. Create a gazetteer listing cities, towns, or counties named after important figures in U.S. or Virginia history.

(copy this activity front-and-back)
- Make a timeline of key events in the life of a fictitious immigrant to Virginia from one of the two groups you researched.
- Write a journal entry as an immigrant to Virginia today. What similarities do you share with immigrants of the past? How is being an immigrant easier today than 100 years ago? How is it harder?

(copy this activity front-and-back)
- What do you wish someone would invent? Maybe that someone is you! Describe your invention. Explain what it would do and the benefit it would provide. How might it work? What would you name it?
- Create an acrostic using the word "Invent," listing important characteristics of inventors.
- Look up and write the definitions of "invention" and "innovation." How are they similar? How are they different? Today, they are often used interchangeably. Why?

Tip: The next six activities can be used to study many different events in Virginia history, as well as the people and places involved. You can choose which events (and people) to focus on as a class, and which to let students choose from for independent work. You can also decide when to use the timeline, cause-and-effect chart, 5-Ws brochure, or biography activity pages, as they are easily adapted to many different events.

Virginia History = U.S. History 37-38
(copy this activity front-and-back)
- Write a journal entry as a participant in the event you selected.
- Connect an event in Virginia history with an issue facing Virginia or the U.S. today. What can we learn from the past that might help us resolve our problem today?

Virginia Timeline 39
(copy this activity single-sided)
- Write about the connections between events on your timeline.
- Describe the period of time between two events on your timeline. What was occurring? What was life like then? Were things getting better or worse? From what perspective?

Virginia History Dig Site. 40
(copy this activity single-sided)
- Choose something unusual or surprising about the site you selected (or about the people who lived there). Write a tour guide script to share this information.
- Research and write the definitions of "historic," "archaeology," and "preservation."

An Important Event in Virginia History 41-42
Ideas: Establishment of Jamestown Colony; First Battle of Manassas; Public Schools Desegregation
(copy this activity front-and-back)
Describe how this historical event influenced future generations and Virginia today. How might our state be different today had this event not occurred or ended differently?

Who Am I? Virginia Edition. 43
(copy this activity single-sided)
- Write a letter to the person you selected. Tell them what you most admire about them, what you found most interesting about them, and what you wish you could ask them.
- What might you one day want to be famous for? Make an action plan to achieve it.

Colorful Virginians 44
(copy this activity single-sided)
- What characteristics do you think of as describing a "colorful" person? How is "colorful" positive? How could "colorful" be negative? List three ways you are "colorful."
- Describe how you contribute, or will one day contribute, to Virginia.

Virginia GOVERNMENT

Virginia Government 45-46
(copy this activity front-and-back)
Tip: Research and discuss the process of how a bill becomes a law in Virginia, as a class. Students could devote a whole spread in their Interactive Notebooks to this topic.
- Write an idea for a new Virginia law. Explain who it would benefit and how.
- Draw a flowchart showing the steps for making a new Virginia law, from introduction of a bill through signing the bill into law.

Virginia Constitution 47
(copy this activity single-sided)
- Suggest a new right or protection to add to the Virginia Constitution. Explain why it is needed today.
- Flip back and reread your idea for a new Virginia law. Ask yourself, "Is it constitutional?" Explain why it is or is not. Who would make the final determination? When? How?

(copy this activity single-sided)
- Research and write the definitions of "campaign," "precinct," and "absentee ballot."
- List some of the polling stations where people in your town go to vote. List the hours Virginia polling locations are usually open. Describe how these factors encourage or discourage people from fulfilling their civic obligation to vote.

(copy this activity single-sided)
Create a T chart. List the costs and benefits of getting a college degree. Compare notes with classmates and add good ideas you didn't think of to your chart. Underneath, list alternatives to a college degree. It's never too soon to start thinking about the future!

(copy this activity single-sided)
Choose four ways to fill in the blank below, and write an answer for each.
"Describe how _____ in Virginia are making news and having a positive impact."
(women, children, African Americans, Hispanics, Asian Americans, teenagers, girls, men, boys, athletes, teachers, etc.)

Virginia ECONOMICS

(copy this activity single-sided)
Keep an economics diary. List all the goods and services you personally buy, use, or consume in one day. Circle areas where you may be wasteful, if any.

(copy this activity single-sided)
- Suggest a business that someone your age could start. List the natural, human, and capital resources you would need. Describe entrepreneurial skills that would help.
- List the human resources that you personally can offer an employer looking to fill a job.

(copy this activity front-and-back)
List natural, human, and capital resources you see in use at your school. Look for areas where the school is being efficient or inefficient. Write a letter to the principal with suggestions for improvements.

(copy both pages single-sided, each on their own sheet of paper)
Write interview questions you would ask a business owner to learn what makes a business successful. If possible, interview a local business owner, and record his or her responses.

Virginia STATE SYMBOLS

(copy this activity single-sided)
Write the follow-up to this statement (without using information from the baseball card):
"Here's something I bet you didn't know about Virginia:"

(copy this activity single-sided)
- Create a gazetteer listing 10 Virginia monuments in alphabetical order.
- Visit or research a Virginia monument, and write down the inscription from that monument. Describe the thoughts and emotions that inscription inspires in you.

Virginia State Symbols 59-60
(copy this activity front-and-back)

Suggest an idea for a new state symbol. Write a convincing argument for why the symbol would be a great addition and a good representation of Virginia.

Virginia State Flag 61-62
(copy this activity front-and-back)

- List five elements you would include in the design if the Virginia state flag were to be updated today. Explain the meaning of each and why you would include it.
- Research and explain why the Virginia flag is sometimes flown at half-staff. List a time and reason when it was.

Virginia State Seal 63-64
(copy this activity front-and-back)

- Write the Virginia state motto. Then describe what it means. Suggest a new motto, or defend the current motto as still relevant for today.
- Design a seal for yourself. Then list things you could put it on.

Virginia Fanfare. 65-66
(copy both pages single-sided, each on their own sheet of paper)

- Virginia sports fans are often passionate about their teams! List reasons people become fans of certain teams. Why are sports so popular? How does sports unite us?
- Suggest a new mascot for a Virginia sports team, and draw it.

Virginia Claims to Fame 67-68
(copy this activity front-and-back)

- Write copy for an advertisement in a vacation magazine urging people to come to Virginia and enjoy features for which the state is famous.
- Your cousins from out-of-state are coming to visit you. It'll be their first time in Virginia! Where is the #1 place you will you take them? Why?

Tip: Give students a standing assignment to write a sentence or short paragraph about how they are impacted by what they learned. Ideas include:

"What am I really glad I learned, and why?"

"How did what I learned change my perspective?"

"How can I use what I learned?"

"How can I share what I learned?"

"What do I want to learn even more about?"

Virginia Interactive Notebook • ©Carole Marsh/Gallopade • www.gallopade.com • Page 12

INTERACTIVE NOTEBOOK INSTRUCTIONS
LET'S LEARN ABOUT VIRGINIA!

Dear Students,

This year, you will create an Interactive Notebook about Virginia!
You will work on a wide variety of activities as you build your Interactive Notebook. You will apply the concepts and skills we cover in class to transform Interactive Notebook activity pages into unique displays of your knowledge about our state. You will learn about Virginia geography, history, people, government, economics, and symbols. You will explore what unites Virginia with the rest of our nation, and what makes Virginia unique. And, you will extend your thinking beyond the activities to express your opinions, apply knowledge to new scenarios, and reflect on what you learn. *It's going to be a great year!*

Organization: Here is how your Interactive Notebook will be organized. We will review this and set up these pages together in class.

Location	Page Title/Description	Page #
first 7 pages	Personalized Title Page	1
	Table of Contents	2-5
	Interactive Notebook Instructions	6
	Interactive Notebook Rubric	7
middle pages	Your Activities & Work + Unit Pages & KWLs	8-?
last 5 pages	Glossary (add words throught the year)	G1-G5

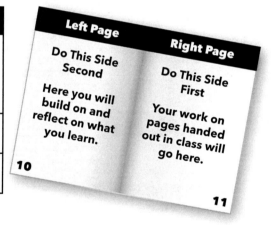

Left Page

Do This Side Second

Here you will build on and reflect on what you learn.

Right Page

Do This Side First

Your work on pages handed out in class will go here.

10

11

Interactive Notebook Requirements:

● Be sure you have your Interactive Notebook and supplies in class each day.

● Your Interactive Notebook should be neat, organized, and up-to-date.

● It is your responsibility to get and make up assignments when you are absent.

● Every time you get a new assignment, add it to the Table of Contents right away.

● Your Interactive Notebook should also be colorful and creative. Highlight and illustrate important terms and concepts. Use color to add pizzazz to your charts, timelines, and activities. You do NOT have to be a great artist to produce a great Interactive Notebook—it's the effort and learning that count.

Activity Key:
gray shading = glue
dashed line = cut
thick solid line = fold

P.S. Read instructions carefully and put care into your work, but don't panic if a paper tears, you cut the wrong lines, or you glue something upside-down. We can tape it, glue it, redo it, or just let it be upside-down—it's definitely NOT the end of the world!

INTERACTIVE NOTEBOOK RUBRIC

This rubric is based on an easy-to-use 10-point scale. Circle points earned in each category and tally at the end.

Student Name: _____   **Date:** _____

CATEGORY	GREAT JOB!	ALMOST THERE	NEEDS WORK
Notebook Organization (max 2 points)	All pages have numbers and titles. Table of contents is up-to-date, neat, and organized. Each unit begins with a KWL chart. KWL charts are updated for completed units.	Missing a few page numbers and titles. The table of contents is up-to-date, and fairly neat and organized. KWL pages are fairly current.	Missing many page numbers and titles. Table of contents is missing many entries and needs to be neater and more organized. KWL pages are missing or incomplete.
Points Earned	2	1	0
Left-Facing Page Assignments (max 4 points)	All assignments to date have been completed. Work is thorough. Writing is detailed and energetic/interesting. Writing and reflection assignments show student is thinking about what is being learned.	Nearly all the assignments to date are completed. Work is fairly thorough. Writing is generally detailed, but could be even better if more time is spent thinking about the material.	Quite a few assignments given in class are missing from the notebook or incomplete. Work needs to be more thorough. Writing needs more detail and energy. Student needs to put more time into thinking about the material.
Points Earned	4	3	1 0
Right-Facing Page Activities (max 4 points)	All activities to date are completed. Work shows creativity and thought. Research tasks show good effort and results. Writing tasks are done with good detail. Coloring, drawing, cutting, and gluing are done neatly. All required notes and labels are present.	Nearly all activities are completed. Work shows some creativity and thought but could use more effort and research. Writing is generally detailed but could be improved. Coloring, drawing, cutting, and gluing are generally good. Most notes and labels are present.	Several activities are missing or incomplete. Coloring, drawing, cutting, and gluing are sometimes sloppy. Notes and labels are missing or incomplete. More effort is needed in research, content, and creativity. Writing needs more detail and energy.
Points Earned	4	3	1 0

Total Points Earned:
(10 possible)

Additional Notes & Comments:

USING MAPS & GLOBES TO LEARN ABOUT VIRGINIA

Maps and globes help us find **where places are located**.
They also help us find out **what places are like**.

Different types of maps show different features and information.
Different types of maps can be used for different purposes.

globe

a round model of Earth; shows major physical and political features

political map

shows political features, such as boundaries and names of countries, states, regions, or cities

physical map

shows physical features, such as bodies of water, mountains, plateaus, etc.

population map

shows areas of high, medium, and low population (where people live)

transportation map

shows highways, roads, airports, and other transportation routes

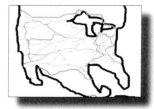

climate map

shows the climate of various areas, including temperature and rainfall

This map shows the world.

This map shows Virginia counties.

This map shows Virginia rivers.

This map shows how much it rains in Virginia.

This map shows highways in Virginia.

This map shows where Virginians live.

This notebook activity is printed single-sided on two different sheets. Parts of each sheet will go in your Interactive Notebook.

1. Cut along the dashed lines on each page.

2. Glue the "Using Maps & Globes ..." title and text to the top of a page in your Interactive Notebook.

3. Fold along the solid lines so the maps are on the outside/top.

4. Glue the six folded maps below the "Using Maps & Globes ..." text.
   (Only put glue on the gray flaps. Make sure each map is face-up.)

5. One map at a time, complete the following steps:
   • Read the description on the folded map.
   • Flip up the folded map.
   • On the back of the flap, write a question about Virginia that could be answered using this type of map.
   • Then, glue the picture of this type of map on the Interactive Notebook page underneath the flap.
   Continue until you complete these steps with all six types of maps.

Activity Key:
gray shading = glue
dashed line = cut
thick solid line = fold

MY MAP OF
VIRGINIA

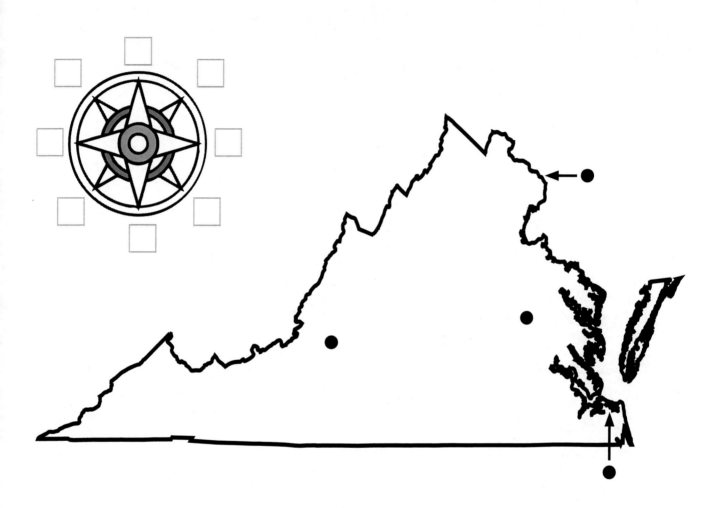

Map Key

This is a two-sided notebook activity.
This entire sheet will go in your Interactive Notebook.

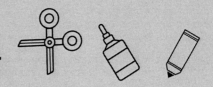

Follow these steps to complete the map on the other side of this sheet.

1. Locate and label Virginia's major cities:
    - **RICHMOND**
    - **ROANOKE**
    - **NORFOLK**
    - **ALEXANDRIA**

2. Which city is Virginia's capital? Draw a ★ on it.

3. Draw a ☻ on the map for the city where you live. Label the city if it is not already labeled.

4. Draw Virginia's major rivers in blue, and label them:
    - **JAMES**
    - **RAPPAHANNOCK**
    - **POTOMAC**

5. Add abbreviations for cardinal and intermediate directions to the compass rose.

6. As you complete your map, create a map key to explain your symbols.

7. Create a symbol for the following physical features and add them to the map and map key.
    - **CHESAPEAKE BAY**
    - **LAKE DRUMMOND**
    - **SHENANDOAH VALLEY**

8. Double-check to be sure you did not miss any steps by finding each item on your map and crossing it off the list on this side of the sheet.

9. Glue your map into your Interactive Notebook. (Put the glue on this side of the sheet.)

REMINDER:
For all activities, gray shading indicates which part of the sheet to put glue on.

VIRGINIA'S PLACE IN THE UNITED STATES

ON THE MAP...

Color Virginia blue.

Color the rest of the states in our region yellow.

This is a two-sided notebook activity.

This entire sheet will go in your Interactive Notebook.

1. Fold this page in half along the solid line, so the map is on the outside.

2. Complete the activities on both sides.

3. Glue the folded sheet to the top of a page in your Interactive Notebook.
   (Only put glue on the gray flap. Make sure the map is face-up.
   The folded edge should be at the bottom.)

4. On the bottom half of your Interactive Notebook page, list characteristics
   that describe your region of the U.S.
   Include natural characteristics and human characteristics.

U.S. REGIONS

A **region** is an area with one or more common, or shared, characteristics. The shared characteristics of a region distinguish it from surrounding areas. Regions are a human construct. That means people choose the criteria by which a region is defined.

An area can be divided into regions in many ways, depending on what criteria are used. Criteria commonly used to determine regions include landforms, climate, economics, language, and culture.

The United States is commonly divided into five regions. These regions are based on shared physical and economic characteristics, as well as historical events and culture. Physical features that create natural boundaries often impact how the regions are divided.

IN THE TEXT ABOVE...
- ☐ Highlight the definition of "region" in yellow.
- ☐ Highlight some characteristics that can be used to define a region in orange.
- ☐ Highlight how physical features affect the way regions are defined in blue.

Virginia is in this U.S. region:

FILL IN THE BLANKS...

1. A _____ is an area with one or more common characteristics.

2. Landforms and economics are _____ that can be used to define a region.

3. _____ between the regions impact how the regions are divided.

This is a one-sided notebook activity.

This whole sheet will go in your Interactive Notebook.

1. Label each region. Then lightly color each region a different color.
2. Fold along the solid line so the map is on the outside.
3. Glue the folded sheet to the top of a page in your Interactive Notebook. (Only put glue on the gray flap.)
4. Flip up the map, and write interesting facts about each region on the Interactive Notebook page underneath.

VIRGINIA REGIONS

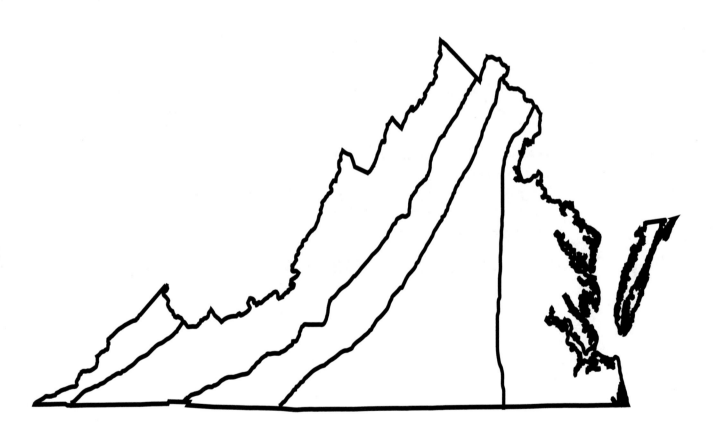

This is a one-sided notebook activity.
This entire page will go in your Interactive Notebook

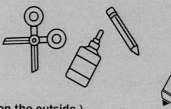

1. Cut along the dashed lines.

2. Fold the page in half along the solid line. ("Virginia Climate" should be on the outside.)

3. Research Virginia's climate. *For example: How hot do summers in Virginia get, and how cold do winters get? How much rain, sleet, or snow does Virginia get each year? How long is Virginia's growing season, and in which months is it? Etc.*

4. On the front of each flap, define the bold term and draw a picture to describe it.

5. Flip up the flaps and write information on the back of each to describe how Virginians adapt.

6. On the sheet underneath the flaps, describe extreme weather conditions and events that Virginia sometimes experiences.

7. Glue this folded sheet to the top half of a page in your Interactive Notebook.
(Only put glue on the gray flap. Make sure the chart is face-up.)

8. On the bottom half of your Interactive Notebook page, create a data table.
Track the weather each day for a week or month.
You can include temperature highs and lows, precipitation, wind speed, or other data.

VIRGINIA CLIMATE

Temperature	Precipitation	Growing Season

VIRGINIA AGRICULTURE

How does Virginia use its land and water? One way is for agriculture!
Agriculture includes growing crops and raising livestock.

Not only do we depend on agriculture for the food we eat, agriculture is essential for the
production of many of our clothes, home textiles, medicines, and even automobile fuel!

This is a one-sided notebook activity.
Part of this sheet will go in your Interactive Notebook.

1. Cut along the dashed lines.

2. Fold along the solid lines. (Fold so all the flaps cover the center "Top Crops" triangle.)

3. With all three triangle flaps folded in, put glue on the back of the center triangle and glue the foldable in your
    Interactive Notebook. (Only put glue on the center triangle, so the flaps still open and close.
    The "Top Crops" triangle should be face up when you unfold the flaps.)

4. Research Virginia agriculture.

5. Start with the foldable unfolded.
    Write the names of three of Virginia's top
    crops, one in each triangle.
    Draw a picture to illustrate each one.

6. Flip over each flap one at a
    time. On the back of each flap,
    list 3 goods that are made
    from that crop.

7. On your notebook
    paper underneath
    the flaps, or at
    the bottom of the
    page, describe
    why each crop
    is successful in
    Virginia.

Virginia Interactive Notebook
©Carole Marsh/Gallopade
www.gallopade.com • Page 23

Activity Key:
gray shading = glue
dashed line = cut
thick solid line = fold

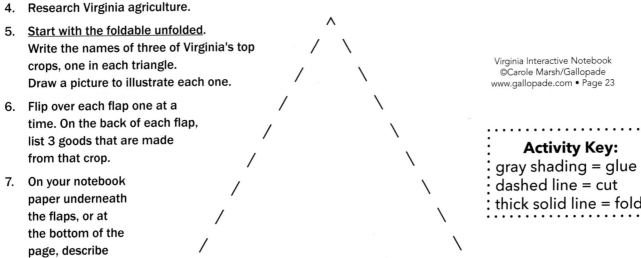

TOP VIRGINIA CROPS

VIRGINIA NATURE

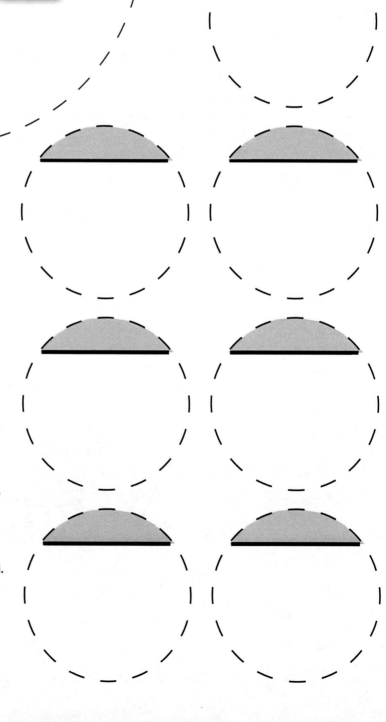

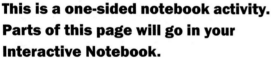

This is a one-sided notebook activity. Parts of this page will go in your Interactive Notebook.

1. Cut along the dashed lines, creating circles.

2. Fold the small circles along the solid lines.

3. Research to learn about Virginia nature. *Learn about some of our abundant or unique mammals, trees, plants, fish, reptiles, etc.*

4. On the front of each small circle (the side with the gray), write the name of a different Virginia plant or animal. Then draw a picture of the plant or animal on the back.

5. Glue the large circle onto the center of a page in your Interactive Notebook.

6. Glue the small circles along the outer edge of the large circle. Only put glue on the gray area, so the small circles flip open and closed. (You can glue them to open inwards or outwards—your choice!)

VIRGINIA TRANSPORTATION

Virginia's transportation system helps move Virginia resources, products, and people throughout the state, and to other parts of the nation and the world!

Map Legend

This is a one-sided notebook activity.

Part of this sheet will go in your Interactive Notebook.

1. On the map, mark sites and routes of important elements of Virginia's transportation system. *Possibilities include interstate highways, airports, truck terminals, railroads, ports, etc.* Label the sites and routes.

2. As you draw your map, create a map legend to explain your symbols.

3. Cut along the dashed line. Then glue this page in your Interactive Notebook.

A FAMOUS VIRGINIAN

Name: _____

Born: _____ Died: _____

Contribution: _____

_____

_____

_____

_____

- -

This is a one-sided notebook activity, but you may use it multiple times.
Most of this sheet will go in your Interactive Notebook.

1. Research a famous Virginian who had a major impact on our state, country, or the world!
2. Complete the picture frame:
    - Draw, or print and glue, a picture of the person you selected.
      (Your illustration could be a portrait or it could show a scene from his or her life.)
    - Fill in the missing details. Describe the contribution made and why it was important.
3. Cut along the dashed line.
4. Glue the picture frame on the top of a page in your Interactive Notebook.
5. Below the picture frame, describe how this Virginian's contribution affects your life today.

AMERICAN INDIANS IN VIRGINIA

This is a two-sided notebook activity. This entire sheet will go in your Interactive Notebook.

1. Fold along the solid lines to create a brochure. ("American Indians in Virginia" is your cover, so it should be on top when folded. The gray section should be on the bottom.)

2. Research two American Indian groups or tribes who lived in Virginia.

3. Write the names of the two groups on the front cover of your brochure.

4. On the inside panels of the brochure, describe how each American Indian group met its needs for food, shelter, and clothing. *What did they eat? How did they get it? Did they live in permanent villages or were they nomadic? How did they dress? Etc.*

5. Describe other aspects of each group's culture, such as celebrations, music, art, and dance, on the "Customs & Traditions" panel.

6. Illustrate the cover and panels of your brochure based on what you learned.

7. Glue the brochure into your Interactive Notebook. (Put glue on the gray panel only.)

Customs & Traditions

Group or Tribe:

Group or Tribe:

Food

Group or Tribe:

Group or Tribe:

Shelter

Group or Tribe:

Group or Tribe:

Clothing

Group or Tribe:

Group or Tribe:

VIRGINIA EXPLORATION

Giovanni da Verrazzano was born around 1485 in Italy. When he was in his early 20s, Verrazzano became interested in a career as a sailor. By the time Verrazzano was in his late 30s, he had traveled to places like Egypt and Syria and built a reputation in Europe as a skilled and brave mariner.

King Francis I of France hired Giovanni da Verrazzano to explore the eastern coast of North America. Like other European leaders, King Francis was eager to find a fast sea route from Europe to Asia to trade for more Asian spices and silks! The king also worried France was falling behind Spain and Portugal in exploring the West and wanted his country to take an important role.

The voyage did not get off to a good start. Giovanni da Verrazzano prepared four ships, but three of them were destroyed by storms or battles with Spanish ships. In January 1524, only a ship called the *Delfina* carried the Verrazzano expedition across the Atlantic.

After 50 days at sea, the men spotted land near what is now called Cape Fear, North Carolina. Giovanni da Verrazzano first steered his ship south. But when he reached the northern part of Florida, he turned the *Delfina* around and headed back north, never losing sight of the coastline.

As the ship kept moving north, Giovanni da Verrazzano and his men drew maps of the North Carolina, Virginia, Maryland, Delaware, New Jersey, New York, Connecticut, Rhode Island, Massachusetts, New Hampshire, and Maine coasts. Along the way, the *Delfina* entered the Bay of New York, and the men came ashore on the southern tip of today's Manhattan Island. Later, they also made landfall at what is now Newport, Rhode Island. After making it as far north as what is now Newfoundland in Canada, the Verrazzano expedition returned to France in July 1524.

A few years later, Giovanni da Verrazzano led another expedition on behalf of France to again seek a swift sea route to the Pacific Ocean. This time, Verrazzano decided to look farther south in North America. Near today's Jamaica, he went ashore on an island along with several crewmen. They were attacked and killed by natives.

Giovanni da Verrazzano is famous for advancing European mapmaker's knowledge of the East Coast of North America. Bridges in New York City and in Rhode Island are named for him.

IN THE TEXT ABOVE...
- ☐ Highlight mentions of cardinal or intermediate directions in yellow.
- ☐ Highlight mentions of bodies of water in blue.
- ☐ Highlight mentions of other features, such as mountains and borders, in green.

This is a one-sided notebook activity.
Glue this entire sheet onto a page in your Interactive Notebook.

GIOVANNI DA VERRAZZANO

This is a one-sided notebook activity.
Two parts of this sheet will go in your Interactive Notebook.

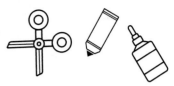

1. Cut along the dashed lines.

2. Color the illustration in the center.

3. Fold along the solid lines. (Fold flaps inward, over the illustration, so the outer corners meet in the center.)

4. Write interesting facts about Giovanni da Verrazzano and his expeditions on both sides of each flap.

5. Glue the foldable to the center of a page in your Interactive Notebook. Glue the title above it.
   (Only put glue behind the center diamond where the picture is, so the flaps still open and close.)

Who?

Who?

Who?

Where?

When?

Why?

Virginia Interactive Notebook
©Carole Marsh/Gallopade
www.gallopade.com • Page 31

This is a two-sided notebook activity.

Part of this sheet will go in your Interactive Notebook.

1. Cut along the dashed lines on the other side of this sheet.

2. Fold along the solid lines. (Fold flaps inward, over the center title.)

3. Glue the foldable in your Interactive Notebook.
    (Just put glue on the gray area, so the flaps still open and close. Be sure the title is face-up.)

Instructions continue on other side...

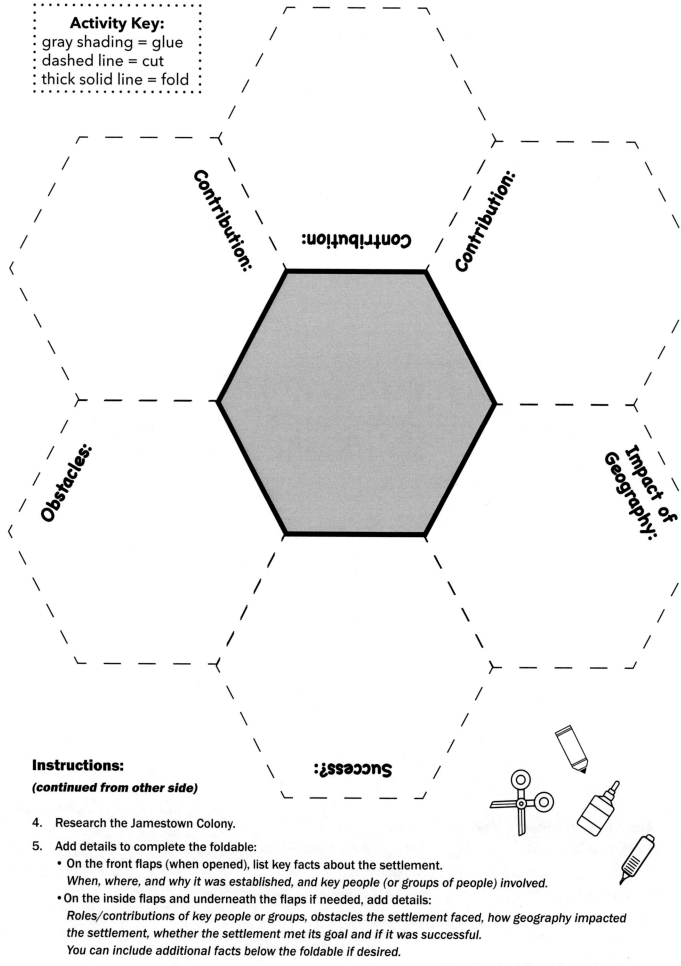

Contribution:

Contribution:

Contribution:

Obstacles:

Impact of Geography:

Success?

Instructions:

(continued from other side)

4. Research the Jamestown Colony.

5. Add details to complete the foldable:
   • On the front flaps (when opened), list key facts about the settlement.
     When, where, and why it was established, and key people (or groups of people) involved.
   • On the inside flaps and underneath the flaps if needed, add details:
     Roles/contributions of key people or groups, obstacles the settlement faced, how geography impacted the settlement, whether the settlement met its goal and if it was successful.
     You can include additional facts below the foldable if desired.

This is a two-sided notebook activity.
This entire sheet will go in your Interactive Notebook.

1. Research two of the immigrant groups that helped shape Virginia history.

2. Cut halfway up the page along the two dashed lines. Stop cutting at the solid line.

3. Fold each flap over on the solid line. (The Venn diagram should be on the outside.)

4. Write the names of two different immigrant groups under "Group 1" and "Group 2".

5. Use the Venn diagram to compare and contrast the two groups. *Include details such as where they came from, where they settled, when they came, why they immigrated here, etc.*

6. Flip up the flaps. On the back of the two outside flaps describe cultural aspects of each of the two groups. *What language did they speak, what religion did they practice, what foods did they eat, and other aspects of their customs and traditions.* On the back of the center flap describe some of Virginia's culture that they would have found new and different than what they were used to.

7. Under the bottom title "Virginia: Our New Home," illustrate how the two groups adapted and contributed to their new home.

8. Glue this sheet on the top half of a page in your Interactive Notebook.
   (Only put glue on the gray flap. Make sure the Venn diagram is face-up.)

9. On the bottom half of your Interactive Notebook page, draw or glue a world map, and identify the countries or locations the two groups of immigrants came from. Then trace their paths to Virginia.

VIRGINIA IMMIGRANTS

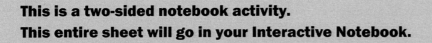

Group 1

Both

Group 2

Virginia: Our New Home!

Group 1
Culture

New
Culture

Group 2
Culture

VIRGINIA INVENTORS

Invention

Inventor

This is a two-sided notebook activity. This sheet will be cut into two pieces. Both parts will go into your Interactive Notebook.

1. Research three inventors from Virginia. They can be from the state's past or present.

2. Cut along the dashed lines.

3. Fold along the solid lines.

4. With the flaps closed, write the name of each inventor on the left outside flap, and write the name of his or her invention on the right outside flap.

5. On the insides of the flaps, glue or draw pictures of each inventor and his or her invention.

6. On the center lines, describe the impact of each invention. *Explain who it helped, how it helped, and how it changed lives.*

7. Glue the "Virginia Inventors" title to the top of a page in your Interactive Notebook.

8. Glue this foldable in your Interactive Notebook, underneath the title.
   (Only put glue on the gray section, so the flaps continue to open and close.)

Invention

Inventor

Activity Key:
gray shading = glue
dashed line = cut
thick solid line = fold

Invention

Inventor

Inventor   **Invention**

_____

_____

_____

_____

_____

_____

_____

Inventor   **Invention**

_____

_____

_____

_____

_____

_____

_____

Inventor   **Invention**

_____

_____

_____

_____

_____

_____

_____

This is a two-sided notebook activity.

This entire sheet will go in your Interactive Notebook.

1. Select one of the events on the list, and highlight it.
2. Research to learn more about that event. Explore how Virginia's people and places were involved. Think about and make inferences to determine how the event impacted Virginians.
3. On the back of this sheet, describe causes, the event, and results in the center boxes.
4. In the bubbles around the event, describe how people and places in Virginia contributed to this event. (You can add extra bubbles if you need to.)
5. Fold along the solid line so the list of events is on the outside.
6. Glue this folded sheet to the top of a page in your Interactive Notebook. (Only put glue on the gray flap.)
7. Flip up the sheet. On your Interactive Notebook page underneath, describe the impact this event had on Virginia and the United States. *For example: What groups of people were affected by the event? How did life change during the event? How did life change after the event? What were positive outcomes? What were any negative outcomes?*

VIRGINIA HISTORY = U.S. HISTORY

Not only does Virginia history include what happened in Virginia, our state history includes the role of Virginia and Virginians in the historic events of the United States!

Virginia has played an important role in all of these events:

- **The Declaration of Independence**
- **The Revolutionary War**
- **Foundations of the U.S., including the U.S. Constitution and Bill of Rights**
- **Territorial Growth and Expansion of the United States**
- **The American Civil War**
- **Reconstruction and Change**
- **American Indian Removal and the Trail of Tears**
- **The Great Movement West**
- **Industrialization and Urbanization**
- **Building of Railroads, Highways, and Airports**
- **Immigration to America**
- **World War I and World War II**
- **The Great Depression and New Deal**
- **The Cold War**
- **America's Civil Rights Movement**
- **Women's Suffrage Movement**
- **Development of a Modern Economy**
- **Development of a Global, Connected Society**
- ***& Lots More!***

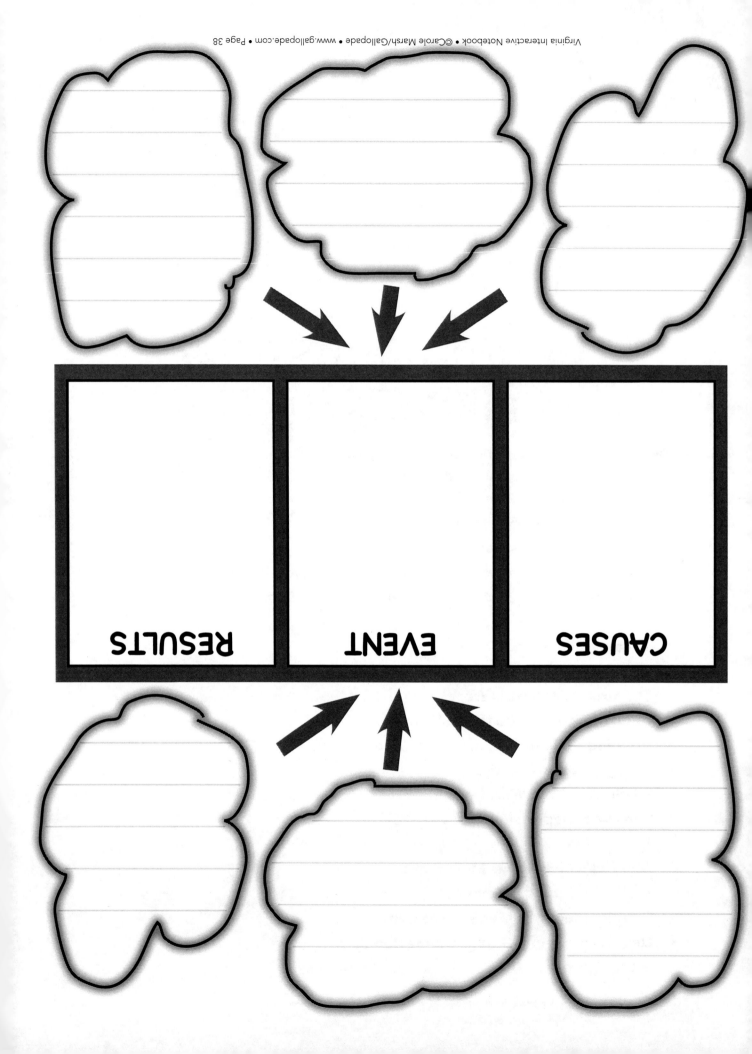

RESULTS

EVENT

CAUSES

VIRGINIA TIMELINE

This is a one-sided notebook activity.

Part of this sheet will go in your Interactive Notebook, glued across two pages.

This activity sheet can be used for many different topics throughout the year.

1. Research an event, as instructed by your teacher.
2. Fill in the timeline squares with text and illustrations about key events.
3. Cut along the dashed lines.
4. Write a title for your timeline, across the top of the sheets.
5. Glue the timeline horizontally across the top of a two-page spread in your Interactive Notebook.
6. Your teacher will tell you what to write about underneath.

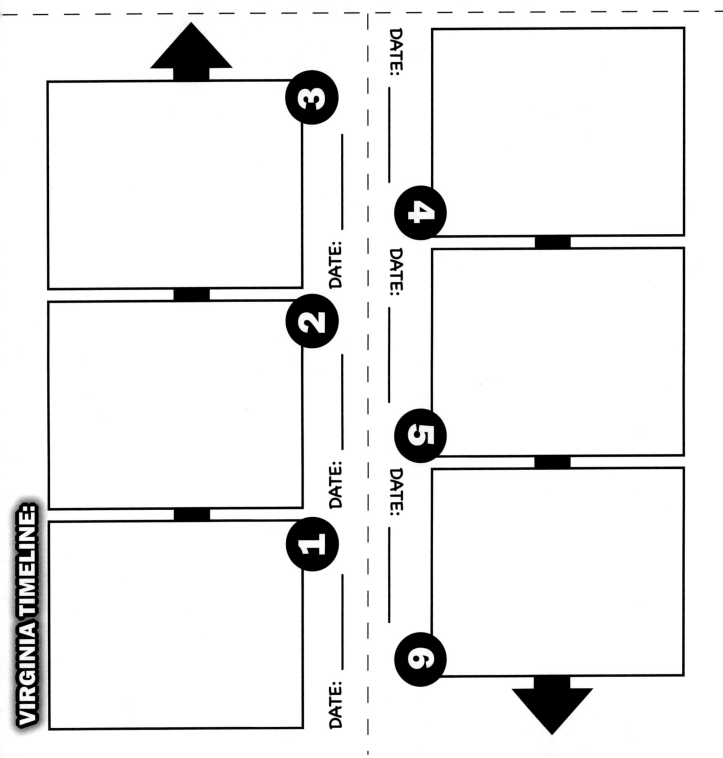

This is a one-sided notebook activity.

This entire sheet will go in your Interactive Notebook.

1. Research an archaeological site, or an old settlement or village, in Virginia.
2. Write the name of the site you are researching in the dotted box.
   On the map of Virginia, draw a star to show where the site is located.
   Then list facts and details about the site based on your research. Describe or draw any artifacts found.
3. Fold along the solid line so the title and facts are on the outside.
4. Glue this folded sheet to the top of a page in your Interactive Notebook. (Only put glue on the gray flap.)
5. Flip up the sheet, and on the back, illustrate what the site looked like long ago. Include artifacts that were found or could be found at your dig site. Underneath, on your Interactive Notebook page, describe what you learned about the people associated with your site. What conclusions do artifacts tell you about their way of life?

VIRGINIA HISTORY DIG SITE

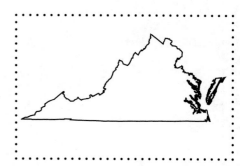

AN IMPORTANT EVENT IN VIRGINIA HISTORY

Who?

What?

This is a two-sided notebook activity.
This entire sheet will go in your Interactive Notebook.
You can use this activity sheet multiple times throughout the year.

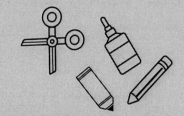

1. Cut along the dashed line.

2. Fold along the solid lines.

3. Research an important event from the history of Virginia. (Your teacher may assign a specific topic.)

4. Create a brochure about the event. On the five panels of the brochure, write about <u>what</u> happened, <u>who</u> was involved, <u>when</u> it occurred, <u>where</u> it took place, and <u>why</u> the event was significant. Add illustrations.

5. Glue the brochure on a page in your Interactive Notebook. (Only put glue on the gray section.)
Glue the "An Important Event..." header above the brochure.

When?

Where?

Why?

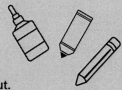

This is a one-sided notebook activity, but you may use it multiple times.
This whole sheet will go in your Interactive Notebook.

1. Select a person from Virginia whom you find interesting or whom you want to know more about.
2. Write interesting facts about this person in the picture frame—but do not write his or her name.
3. Fold along the solid line so the picture frame and facts are on the outside.
4. Glue this sheet to the top of a page in your Interactive Notebook. (Only put glue on the gray flap.)
5. Flip up the sheet. Underneath, write the name of the person, and draw or glue pictures of him/her and things related to his/her life.
6. With the frame closed flat, show your sheet to classmates to see if they can guess "Who am I?"

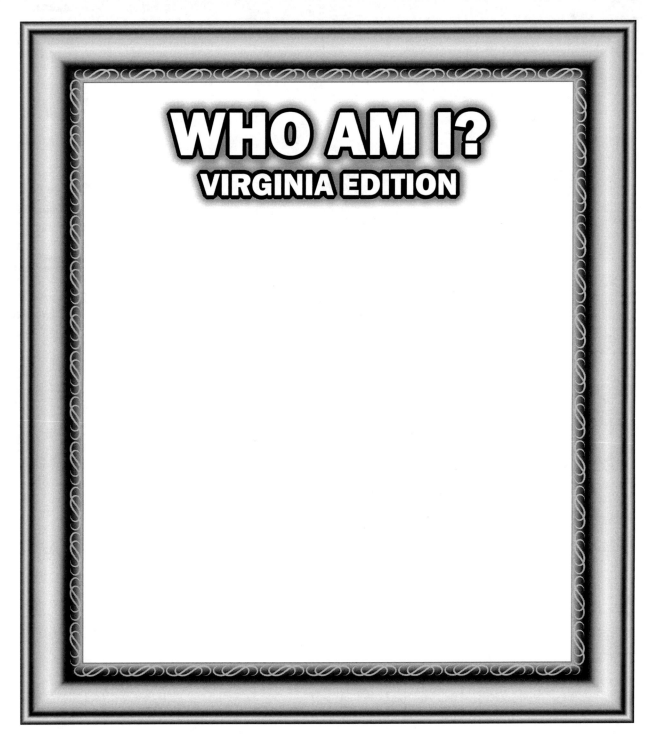

WHO AM I?
VIRGINIA EDITION

COLORFUL VIRGINIANS

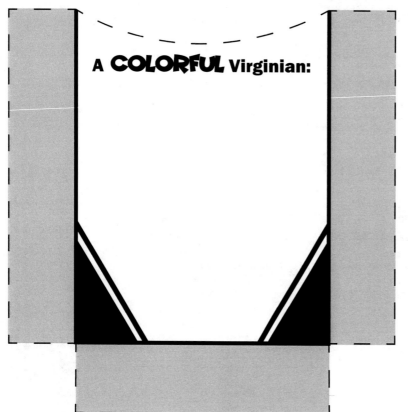

A **COLORFUL** Virginian:

This is a one-sided notebook activity. Parts of this sheet will go in your Interactive Notebook.

1. Choose a Virginia person to research. Write his or her name on the crayon box, and add an illustration of him/her.

2. Write important facts about the person on each crayon.

3. Color each crayon a different color, but only lightly color on the facts.

4. Cut along the dashed lines to cut out the box and crayons.

5. Fold the box along the solid lines.

6. Glue the crayon box in your Interactive Notebook. (Only put glue on the gray flaps. The top of the box should be open.)

7. Slide your crayons in your crayon box.

Add as many colorful Virginians to this Interactive Notebook page as you like!

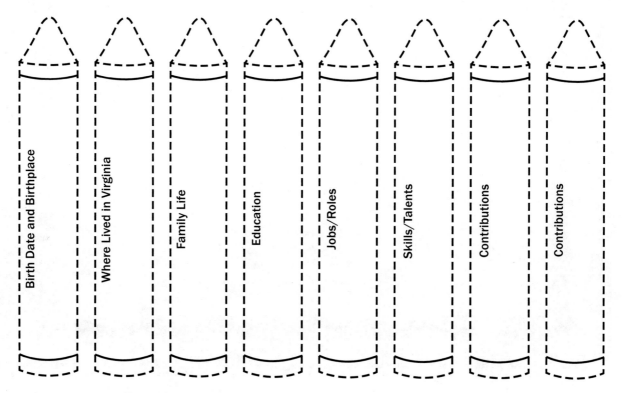

Birth Date and Birthplace

Where Lived in Virginia

Family Life

Education

Jobs/Roles

Skills/Talents

Contributions

Contributions

VIRGINIA STATE GOVERNMENT

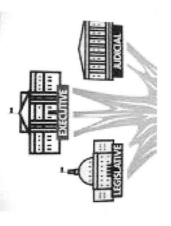

Executive Branch

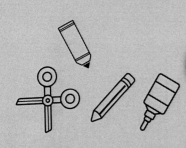

VIRGINIA GOVERNMENT

This is a two-sided notebook activity.
This entire sheet will go in your Interactive Notebook.

1. Cut along the dashed lines.

2. Fold along the solid lines.

3. Research to learn about Virginia's state government.

4. Decorate the front flaps of this sheet with pictures or words that represent each branch of government.

5. Open the flaps, read about Virginia government, and answer the questions.

6. Glue this sheet at the top of a page in your Interactive Notebook.
   Only put glue on the gray area; do not glue the flaps.

7. Once this sheet is glued in your Interactive Notebook, list ways the Virginia state government is similar to the United States federal government and ways it is different. You can write these comparisons on the page surrounding this sheet.

Legislative Branch

Judicial Branch

VIRGINIA'S BRANCHES OF GOVERNMENT

Virginia's three branches of government are established by the state constitution.

Each branch has separate, distinct powers that cannot be taken away by either of the other two branches. Each branch depends on the others to work effectively. This division of authority is called **separation of powers.**

Each branch also has the power to prevent the other branches from overstepping their authority. This protection is known as **checks and balances.**

_____
How long is
his or her term?

_____
Virginia's
executive branch
is led by the

_____
Virginia has
_____
branches of
government.

_____
Virginia's
legislative branch
is called the

**CURRENT
VIRGINIA
LEADERS:**

Governor:
_____

Lieutenant Governor:
_____

Attorney General:
_____

Virginia's
highest court
in the judicial
branch is the
_____

Virginia's highest
court has
_____
justices.

How long is the
term for a
state senator?
_____

How long is the
term for a
state delegate?
_____

How long is the
term for a
justice on
Virginia's
highest court?
_____

VIRGINIA CONSTITUTION

The **U.S. Constitution** is one of our country's most important documents.

The **Virginia Constitution** is one our state's most important documents.

Each constitution establishes a government, provides the structure for how that government operates, identifies government's key responsibilities, sets limits on what the government can do, and tells for whose benefit the government exists.

A **preamble** is an introduction. The preamble of an important document usually identifies on whose authority and for what purpose the document was created. The U.S. Constitution begins with a preamble. The Virginia Constitution does too!

IN THE TEXT ABOVE...
- ☐ Highlight several ways the U.S. and Virginia constitutions are similar in blue.
- ☐ Highlight one way they are different in yellow.
- ☐ Highlight a synonym for "preamble" in pink.

Preamble of the Virginia Constitution

A DECLARATION OF RIGHTS made by the good people of Virginia in the exercise of their sovereign powers, which rights do pertain to them and their posterity, as the basis and foundation of government.

This is a one-sided notebook activity. Parts of this sheet will go in your Interactive Notebook.

1. Cut along the dashed lines.

2. Glue the top part of this page onto the top half of a page in your Interactive Notebook.

3. Fold along the solid line of the preamble.

4. Glue the preamble to the bottom half of your Interactive Notebook page so it is face up and can flip up. Only put glue on the gray flap.

5. Flip up the preamble. On the Interactive Notebook page underneath, explain in your own words what the preamble of the state constitution says.

6. Research how many times the Virginia Constitution has been amended. Write that information on the bottom half of your Interactive Notebook page, to the side of the preamble.

I'M A VIRGINIA VOTER!

One day you will be old enough to vote. But first, you need to register!

STATE OFFICIAL VOTER REGISTRATION FORM

You are not qualified to vote if you have been convicted of a felony and have not received a restoration of voting rights. You may apply to the Governor to restore your voting rights.

Qualifications	1. Are you a citizen of the United States? ☐Yes ☐No 2. Will you be 18 years of age on or before Election Day? ☐Yes ☐No

If you answered "No" to either of these questions, do not complete this form.

ID Number Provide your driver's license, non-operator ID number, or the last 4 digits of your Social Security number if you have one.	☐ driver's license #: __ __ __ __ __ __ __ __ __ ☐ non-operator ID #: __ __ __ __ __ __ __ __ __ ☐ Last 4 digits of Social Security number: XXX – XX – __ __ __ __ ☐ I do not have a driver's license, non-operator ID, or Social Security number.
Additional Information Date of birth and sex are required.	**Date of Birth** (month, day, year) __ __ / __ __ / __ __ __ __ **Sex** ☐ Male ☐ Female **Phone and/or Email** (optional)
Your Name	**Last** **First** **Middle** **Suffix**
Address Where You Live	**Street Address** (include apt., lot, etc.) **City** **Zip** **County** **If homeless or you do not have an established residence, describe where you reside:**
Where You Receive Mail (if different)	**Address/P.O. Box** **City** **State** **Zip**
Previous Voter Registration Information	**Your name was** **Your address was** **Your city and state were** **Your zip was**
Political Affiliation (check only one)	**Political Parties:** ☐ Democratic ☐ Libertarian ☐ Republican ☐ No Party **Non-Party Political Organizations:** ☐ Green
WARNING If you sign this form and you know the information is not true, you may be convicted of perjury and fined up to $7,500 and/or jailed for up to 5 years.	**Registrant Affidavit** I swear or affirm under penalty of perjury that: • I am the person named above. • I am a citizen of the United States. • I have not been convicted of a felony (or I have received a restoration of rights). • I am at least 17 ½ years old. • I live at the address listed above. • I am not currently judged by a court to be "incompetent to vote." • I do not claim the right to vote anywhere else. **Signature** **Date**

This is a one-sided notebook activity.
Parts of this sheet will go in your Interactive Notebook.

1. Fill out as much of this voter registration form as you can.
2. Cut along the dashed lines.
3. Glue the title and the completed form on a page in your Interactive Notebook.

VIRGINIA COLLEGES

This is a one-sided notebook activity.

Part of this page will go in your Interactive Notebook.

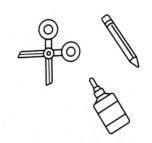

1. Research a Virginia college or university.

2. Write key facts inside the diploma.

3. Decorate the diploma, using the school colors. Sign it.

4. Cut along the dashed line.

5. Glue the diploma onto a page in your Interactive Notebook.

Create diplomas for as many Virginia colleges or universities as you would like!

Diploma

Name of College:

Team Mascot:

Year Founded:

Popular Degree Programs:

Location:

Famous Alumni:

Number of Students:

_____

Signed, Possible Future Graduate

CURRENT EVENTS IN VIRGINIA

TODAY'S NEWS
Look what's happening in our state!

News reported by: _____

☆ ☆ _____ ☆ ☆

_____

_____

_____

_____

_____

_____

_____

_____

This is a one-sided notebook activity.

Part of this sheet will go in your Interactive Notebook.

1. Learn about current events in Virginia.
2. Create your own newspaper front page by writing about one of the biggest or most interesting current events. Include the who, what, when, where, and why of the event.
3. Cut along the dashed line.
4. Glue your newspaper on a page in your Interactive Notebook.

VIRGINIA ECONOMICS

Goods are <u>things</u> people buy or sell to meet needs and wants.
Services are <u>activities</u> people buy or do to meet needs and wants.

Producers make goods and provide services. **Consumers** buy goods and services. Producers sell goods and services to earn income or profit. Consumers buy goods and services to meet their needs and wants. People can be both consumers and producers!

IN THE TEXT ABOVE...
☐ Highlight the definition of "goods" in pink.
☐ Highlight the definition of "services" in blue.
☐ Highlight the reason why producers make goods and provide services in green.
☐ Highlight the reason why consumers buy goods and services in yellow.

This is a one-sided notebook activity.
Parts of this sheet will go in your Interactive Notebook.

1. Cut along the dashed line above. Glue the top piece of this sheet in your Interactive Notebook at the top of a page.
2. Draw a T-chart underneath the sheet. Label one column of the chart Goods, and label the other column Services.
3. Cut out the goods and services below. As you do, glue each rectangle in the correct column of the T-chart.
4. In the blank rectangles, list other goods and services popular in Virginia, and draw pictures of them. Glue those rectangles into the correct column in the T-chart too.

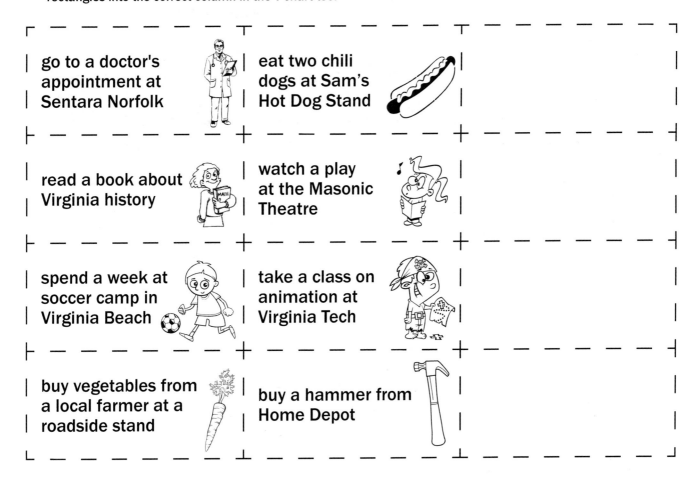

PRODUCTIVE RESOURCES

Resources are things people can use to meet their needs or to produce goods or services. Resources are also called **productive resources**.

Three types of productive resources are frequently used to produce goods and services:

Natural Resources   **Human Resources**   **Capital Resources**

A fourth type of productive resource combines the other resources to produce goods and services. This resource is known as: **Entrepreneurship**

❶ Natural resources are resources that occur naturally (in nature) and can be used to meet needs or to produce goods and services. They are usually found in, on, or around Earth. Examples include trees, minerals, water, and fertile soil. Climate, animals for hunting, and fish in rivers and oceans are also natural resources.

    Example: Natural resources of iron and coal are used to make steel, which is used to make cars.

❷ Human resources are the time and effort people spend to make goods or provide services. Human resources include the training, talents, and skills people use. Human resources are both physical and mental. All goods and services include human labor.

    Example: The labor to design a restaurant and the labor to build it are human resources.
      So is the labor to cook the meals, serve the customers, and wash the dishes.

❸ Capital resources, sometimes called capital goods, are items that are used to produce other goods and services, but that do not become part of the good or service produced. These include machinery, tools, and buildings.

    Example: A grocery store building as well as the racks, refrigerators, cash registers,
      and other equipment used in operating the grocery store are all capital resources.

❹ Entrepreneurship is also an important productive resource. Entrepreneurs combine resources to produce goods and services. Entrepreneurs take risks to bring new ideas to the market, in hopes of earning a profit. Entrepreneurs make decisions about what to produce, for whom to produce, and how to produce. They decide how to use the other resources.

    Example: A toy store owner is an entrepreneur.

IN THE TEXT ABOVE...

☐ Highlight the definition of "natural resources" in orange. Underline examples in orange.
☐ Highlight the definition of "human resources" in yellow. Underline examples in yellow.
☐ Highlight the definition of "capital resources" in blue. Underline examples in blue.
☐ Highlight the definition of "entrepreneurship" in pink. Underline examples in pink.

This is a one-sided notebook activity.
Glue this entire page in your Interactive Notebook.

This is a two-sided notebook activity.
This entire sheet will go in your Interactive Notebook.

1. Cut along the dashed lines. (Stop cutting at the solid line.)

2. Fold each flap over on the solid line.
    (Entrepreneurship should be on the inside.)

3. On the front of each flap, define the type of resource listed.

4. On the back of each flap, list or draw examples of that type of resource.

5. Under "Entrepreneurship," describe how Virginia entrepreneurs use natural, human, and capital resources. Then draw a picture to illustrate how an entrepreneur uses productive resources to produce goods or services right here in Virginia.

6. Glue this sheet to the top of a page in your Interactive Notebook. Make sure the chart is face-up.

7. On the bottom half of your Interactive Notebook page, list several entrepreneurs in Virginia. Include entrepreneurs of large businesses and entrepreneurs of small businesses.

Activity Key:
gray shading = glue
dashed line = cut
thick solid line = fold

VIRGINIA PRODUCTIVE RESOURCES

Natural Resources

Definition:

_____

_____

_____

_____

_____

Human Resources

Definition:

_____

_____

_____

_____

_____

Capital Resources

Definition:

_____

_____

_____

_____

_____

Entrepreneurship

Virginia entrepreneurs
put it all together!

_____

_____

_____

_____

_____

_____

_____

VIRGINIA BUSINESSES SPIN THE WHEEL OF FORTUNE

Virginia businesses are great for our state economy! Virginia businesses provide goods and services that help Virginia consumers meet their needs and wants. Virginia businesses provide jobs that Virginia citizens work at to earn income. Virginia businesses pay taxes that help provide public services for people who live in Virginia.

 IN THE TEXT ABOVE...
☐ Highlight things Virginia businesses provide that help our state.

This notebook activity is two sheets, each printed on one side.
Part of both sheets will go in your Interactive Notebook.
See instructions on the other sheet.

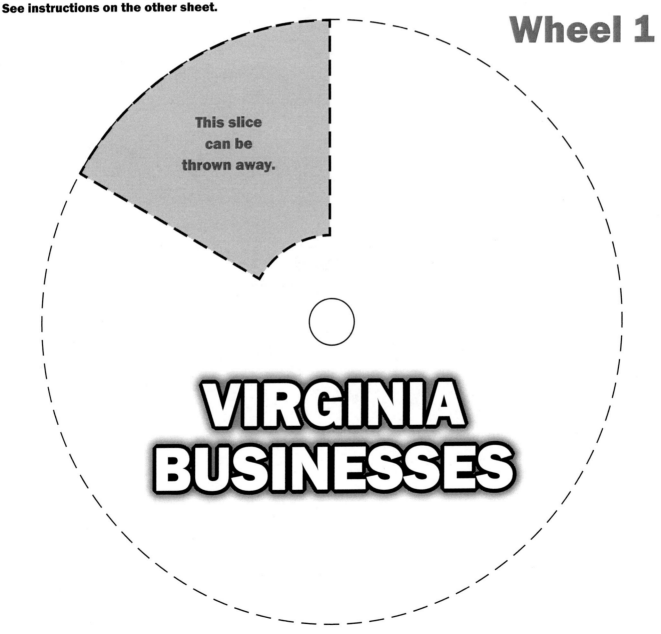

Wheel 1

This slice can be thrown away.

VIRGINIA BUSINESSES

This notebook activity is two sheets, each printed on one side. Part of both sheets will go in your Interactive Notebook.

1. Read the text and do the activity above Wheel 1.

2. Decorate Wheel 1 with things that represent business to you.

3. In the outer rings of Wheel 2, write the names of six Virginia businesses. In each pie-shaped slice, list important facts about that business, including its significance to Virginia.

4. Cut along the dashed lines on both sheets.

5. Glue the text activity to the top of a page in your Interactive Notebook.

6. Glue Wheel 2 in your Interactive Notebook, below the text activity.

7. Place Wheel 1 face-up on top of Wheel 2, lining up the edges of the two wheels. <u>Carefully</u> punch a hole through the center of the two wheels and the Interactive Notebook page. Put a brad through the hole and fold the brad clasps flat against the back of the Interactive Notebook page.

8. Now you can spin your wheel of fortune to reveal information about businesses in Virginia!

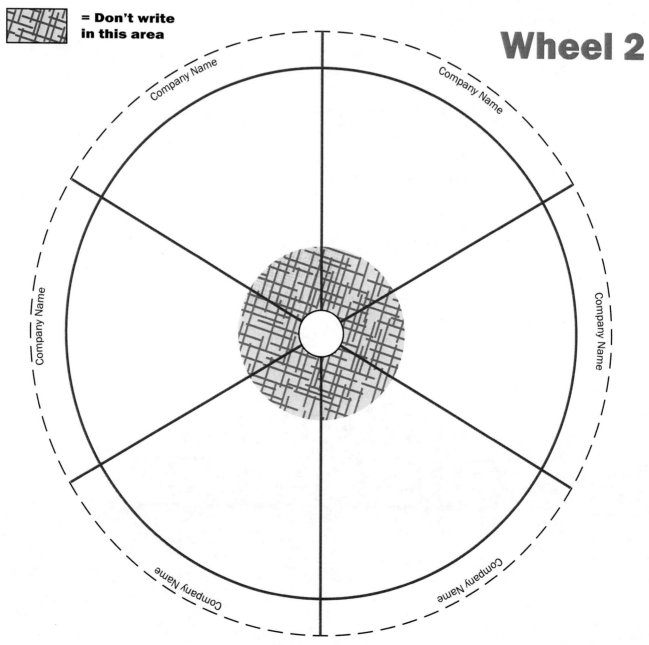

= **Don't write in this area**

Wheel 2

Company Name

VIRGINIA STATS

STATE ABBREVIATION:

SIZE IN SQUARE MILES:

STATEHOOD DATE:

HIGHEST POINT:

CAPITAL CITY:

DISTANCE EAST-TO-WEST

LARGEST CITY:

DISTANCE NORTH-TO-SOUTH

NUMBER OF COUNTIES:

STATE SONG:

CURRENT POPULATION:

STATE MOTTO:

NATIONAL RANK IN POPULATION:

STATE NICKNAME:

This is a one-sided notebook activity.
Part of this sheet will go in your Interactive Notebook.

Baseball cards include key stats about a baseball player.
You can make a "baseball card" for Virginia that lists key stats about the state!

1. Research and add Virginia stats under each heading.

2. Cut along the dashed line.

3. Glue your Virginia Stats "Baseball Card" in your Interactive Notebook.

VIRGINIA MONUMENTS

A **monument** is a building, structure, or place that is created or set aside to recognize important people or events. Some monuments are structures or buildings built specifically as monuments. Some monuments are structures or buildings that become important later because they are unique or important in some way. Some monuments are not human-made at all. For example, the U.S. government has designated a number of beautiful natural areas as national monuments. No matter what their form, monuments are special!

IN THE TEXT ABOVE...
- ☐ Highlight the definition of monument in yellow.
- ☐ Underline the purpose of monuments with a pencil or pen.
- ☐ Highlight three categories of monuments in orange.

(Glue this along the right edge of your Interactive Notebook page.)

_____

_____

_____

_____

_____

_____

_____

_____

_____

Place
Stamp
Here

This is a one-sided notebook activity.
Parts of this sheet will go in your Interactive Notebook.

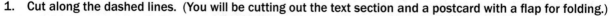

1. Cut along the dashed lines. (You will be cutting out the text section and a postcard with a flap for folding.)
2. Complete the "Monuments" text activity and glue it to the top of a page in your Interactive Notebook.
3. Select a monument in Virginia. It can be large or small, human-made or natural, famous or little known.
4. On the blank side of the postcard, write the name of the monument and draw a picture of it.
5. On the side of the postcard with lines, describe where the monument is, why it is significant, and what/who it helps you remember or think about. You can also address it to someone by filling in the right side.
6. Fold the postcard along the solid line. Then glue your postcard, picture face-out, in your Interactive Notebook. (Only put glue on the gray flap so the postcard can flip open when you want to read the back.)

State Flower

State Insect

State Tree

State Bird

VIRGINIA STATE SYMBOLS

This is a two-sided notebook activity.
Part of this sheet will go in your Interactive Notebook.

1. Cut along the dashed lines.

2. Fold along the solid lines.

3. Draw or glue pictures of state symbols on this side of the flaps.

4. On the inside of each flap, write the name of the state symbol and facts about it. You can include facts about why it is a state symbol or other facts about the animal or thing that is the symbol.

5. Glue this sheet in your Interactive Notebook.
(Only put glue on this gray section, so the flaps open and close.)

6. You can list other state symbols around this foldable on your Interactive Notebook page.

State Insect

State Flower

State Insect Facts

State Flower Facts

State Bird Facts

VIRGINIA SYMBOLS

State Tree Facts

State Bird

State Tree

VIRGINIA STATE FLAG

Virginia's state flag is an important state symbol. It represents Virginia and all its citizens. Every feature on the state flag has meaning—nothing is there by accident!

As a state changes over time, sometimes the state flag is changed too. Elected officials and citizens work together to design a flag that represents the state well.

What do the colors represent?

What do the symbols represent?

What do the words represent?

In what year was the current flag adopted?

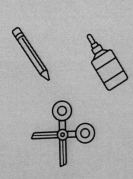

This is a two-sided notebook activity.
Parts of this sheet will go in your Interactive Notebook.

1. Cut along the dashed lines.

2. Glue the title to the top of a page in your Interactive Notebook.

3. Fold along the solid line, so the flaps temporarily cover part of the flag.

4. Research to learn about the Virginia flag.

5. Read the question on each flap. Then flip it over and write the answer to the question on the back.

6. Glue this flag in your Interactive Notebook, just slightly under the title. (Only put glue on the gray area, so the flaps still open and close.)

7. Underneath the flag, write the pledge to the Virginia flag.

Activity Key:
gray shading = glue
dashed line = cut
thick solid line = fold

VIRGINIA STATE SEAL

Virginia has an official state seal. Virginia's state seal includes words and pictures that represent the state. However, a seal is much more than just a decoration. Throughout history, seals have provided evidence that letters, contracts, charters, diplomas, and other official documents are authentic.

 How is the Virginia state seal used today?

_____

_____

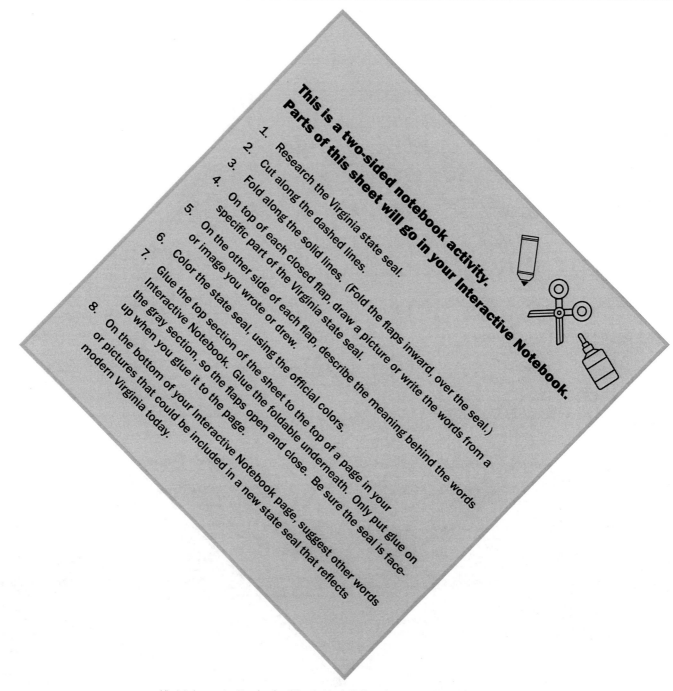

**This is a two-sided notebook activity.
Parts of this sheet will go in your Interactive Notebook.**

1. Research the Virginia state seal.

2. Cut along the dashed lines.

3. Fold along the solid lines. (Fold the flaps inward, over the seal.)

4. On top of each closed flap, draw a picture or write the words from a specific part of the Virginia state seal.

5. On the other side of each flap, describe the meaning behind the words or image you wrote or drew.

6. Color the state seal, using the official colors.

7. Glue the top section of the sheet to the top of a page in your Interactive Notebook. Glue the foldable underneath. Only put glue on the gray section, so the flaps open and close. Be sure the seal is face-up when you glue it to the page.

8. On the bottom of your Interactive Notebook page, suggest other words or pictures that could be included in a new state seal that reflects modern Virginia today.

VIRGINIA FANFARE

My Favorite Team:

_____

Sport:

_____

Team Mascot:

This notebook activity is printed one-sided on two different sheets. Parts of both sheets will go in your Interactive Notebook.

1. Cut out the 12 fan-tabs along the dashed lines. (Two are extras.)

2. Use a hole-punch to punch a hole in the circle of each fan-tab.

3. On the first five fan-tabs, list five sports teams from our state. (The teams can be college or professional, and they can play any sport.) Then illustrate each of these tabs with the team's colors and logo.

4. On the second five fan-tabs, list facts about each team such as its hometown, mascot, and important players—one tab per team.

5. Arrange the fan-tabs where each tab with a team name is followed immediately by that team's facts.

6. Use a hole-punch to punch a hole in the top part of a page in your Interactive Notebook. Use a brad to connect all of the tabs to your notebook page. Once you have done that, you can open and close all of the tabs as though they are part of a fan.

7. Write the name and sport of your favorite team on the extra piece of this activity sheet, and draw or glue a picture of the team's mascot.

8. Cut along the dashed line. Glue the "favorite team" sheet to the same page you attached your fan to in your Interactive Notebook.

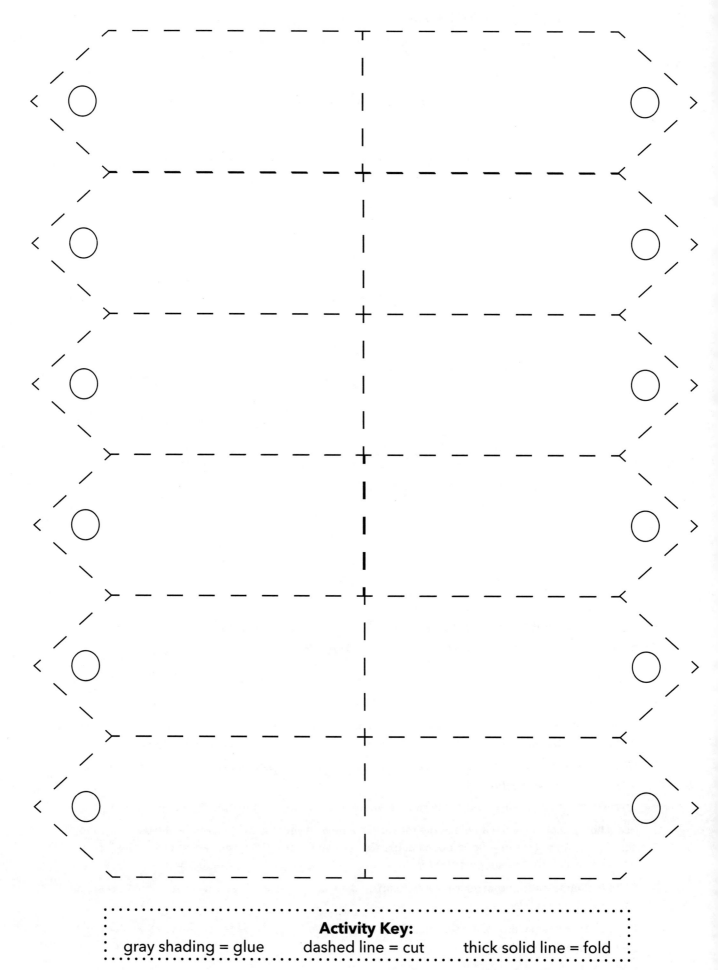

Activity Key:
gray shading = glue   dashed line = cut   thick solid line = fold

VIRGINIA CLAIMS TO FAME

Every state is known for something. It might be natural features such as its beautiful beaches, snowy mountains, fascinating caverns, or hidden bayous. It might be human features such as its sculptures, carvings, wooden bridges, historic downtowns, bustling big cities, and more. It might be cultural features such as its friendly people, artists and musicians, unique architecture, or spicy style of food.

What is Virginia known for? What are some of our "Claims to Fame"?

WHY		WHAT
WHY	**This is a two-sided notebook activity.** **Parts of this sheet will go in your Interactive Notebook.** 1. Cut along the dashed lines. 2. Fold along the solid lines. ("WHAT" and "WHY" should be face out.) 3. Research to learn about three things for which Virginia is particularly famous.	**WHAT**
WHY	4. Complete the outside of each foldable as follows: • List something Virginia is famous for on the WHAT flap. • Explain why Virginia is famous for it on the WHY flap. 5. Complete the inside of each foldable as follows: • Draw or glue pictures of the claim to fame on each inside flap. • Think about what you would tell someone who is not from Virginia and write what you would want them to know. *This could be fascinating facts about our claim to fame, how we became famous for it, why we are so great at it, why being famous for it is great, or anthing else you want to share.*	**WHAT**
WHY	6. Glue the title on the top of a page in your Interactive Notebook. Then glue each foldable underneath the title, on the same page. (Only put glue on the gray area so the flaps still open and close.) **If you want to include more than three great things about Virginia, ask your teacher for extra copies, or just make your own foldables using one of these as a pattern.**	**WHAT**

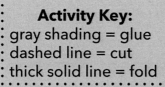

Activity Key:
gray shading = glue
dashed line = cut
thick solid line = fold